A Book Takes Root

A Book Takes Root
The Making of a Picture Book

by Michael Kehoe

Carolrhoda Books, Inc./Minneapolis

The author would like to thank everyone who contributed their time and expertise to the preparation of this book: Elizabeth Thomas, Writer; Vicki Jo Redenbaugh, Artist; Gwenyth Swain, Editor, Carolrhoda Books, Inc.; Gary Hansen, Production Manager, Lerner Publications, Co.; Ken Nelson, Designer; Paul Hunt, P & H Photocomposition; Kim Orne, Typesetter; Jessie Lohman, Keyliner; Curt Tomhave, Meyers Printing Co.; Mike Kohn, Stripper; Randy Jennings, Head Pressman, John Roberts Printing, Inc.; Greg Swanson, Press Operator; Mike Ertle and Jerry Hanson, Muscle Bound Bindery, Inc. Thanks also to editor Lisa Kee for her unfailing interest and dedication to this project.

Publisher's Note: Every publisher works a little differently from every other, and the same holds true for typographers and printers. Add to that the different ways in which individuals work and the different machinery that can be used to do the same jobs, and you come up with any number of variations on the theme of how a book is made. *A Book Takes Root* shows but one variation. For the sake of simplicity and clarity, the others have not been dealt with in this book.

This book is available in two editions:
Library binding by Carolrhoda Books, Inc.
Soft cover by First Avenue Editions
c/o The Lerner Group
241 First Avenue North
Minneapolis, MN 55401

LIBRARY OF CONGRESS CATALOGING-IN-PUBLICATION DATA

Kehoe, Michael.
   A book takes root : the making of a picture book / by Michael Kehoe.
      p.   cm.
   Summary: Traces the process of making a picture book, from idea to manuscript to final publication.
   ISBN 0-87614-756-2 (lib. bdg.)
   ISBN 0-87614-847-X (pbk.)
   1. Picture books for children — Publishing — United States — Juvenile literature. [1. Picture books — Publishing. 2. Books. 3. Authorship.] I. Title.
Z286.P53K44 1993
070.5'0973 — dc20   92-32534
                                                 CIP
                                                 AC

Manufactured in the United States of America

2 3 4 5 6 P/MP 98 97 96 95 94

I would like to dedicate this book to my daughter, Becca, and to my son, Ben. Your early enchantment with books is certain to lead you toward many rewarding adventures.
M.K.

Contents

If your home is anything like mine, you have books all over. Books on tables, books on chairs, books under the bed, books blocking the stairs. With so many books everywhere, they may not seem any more special to you than yesterday's lunch or tomorrow's bus ride.

But they are. Books are special.

In your own hands you can hold an idea and bring it into your mind and into your heart. Because somewhere, maybe in a home just like yours, someone had an idea they wanted to share.

In this book, you're going to see how a book is made. You will see an idea become a shared idea . . . become a book.

The Author

An Idea Becomes A Story

Before there's a cover, or paper, or pictures, or words, there is an idea. And it's an idea that shapes a book, that gives it life. But what comes before an idea? What creates an idea?

First you need an author. The book we're going to follow through the publishing process is called *Green Beans*. It was written by Betsy Thomas. Betsy wasn't an author before *Green Beans*, although she loved children's books and read them often. She worked in an office and lived in an apartment with lots of plants. She learned to love plants from her grandmother.

When Betsy was a little girl, her grandmother would take her out to her garden and explain all the mysteries of seeds and planting, of watering (not too much!) and weeding. She encouraged Betsy to dig in the soil with her bare hands. She shared with her the thrill of finding new seedlings bursting through the soil, reaching for the sun.

Years later, after she became a grown-up, Betsy often recalled the pleasure she had in the garden with her grandmother. She wanted to share her feelings about that time in her life. Since she liked to write, she decided to put her thoughts and feelings into words by writing a children's story.

She took a pad of paper, a special pen, and settled back in her favorite reading spot. Then she thought. And she fiddled. And

she chewed on her pen. No story yet. She made herself a cup of tea—maybe that would help. Now she thought again, and thought and thought until her brain hurt (or so it seemed!).

Still no story. Just vines...creeping onto her page. Slipping from the wallpaper behind her chair and curling into her memories. Vines...grandmother's vines. That's it! That's the story.

Now Betsy was excited. She had a story to tell and she began to write. As soon as one notepad was filled she started another. When the story didn't sound quite right, she tore off the page and kept on going. Winter came and chilled her enthusiasm. To get fresh ideas, she visited plant nurseries. There she could see flowers blooming and touch the soil and smell the fragrances. Inspired, she continued writing.

When the first draft of *Green Beans* was finished, she transferred the story from her hard-to-read notebooks to a computer. The computer printed the story without all the crossing-out marks, lines, and arrows. Then she rewrote the story a second time, and a third time. Each time the story got better. She asked a friend to read it and give her suggestions if something wasn't clear. Finally she was finished and ready to send her story to a children's **book publisher**.

At the Publisher

Let's Make It a Book!

When the *Green Beans* **manuscript** arrived at the children's book publishing company, it was read by an **editor**. Thousands of new book manuscripts are sent to the book publisher each year, and editors decide which ones they'd like to make into books. The editor who read *Green Beans* liked it right away. She showed it to the **publisher** (the head of the company) and the people in charge of selling the books. After everyone had a chance to read and discuss it, they agreed that *Green Beans* would make a fine book. The publishing company acquired the manuscript from Betsy and set to work.

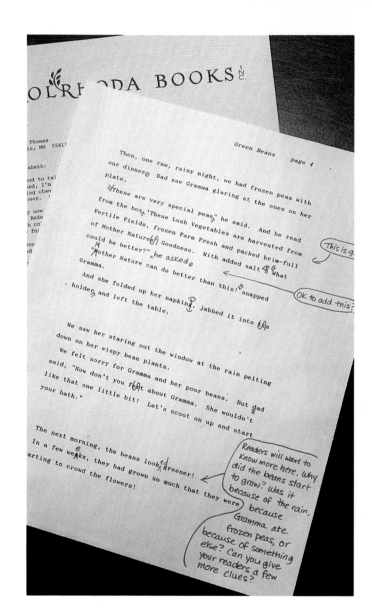

Now the editor goes over the story very carefully to check it for mistakes. Sometimes there are spelling errors or places where the story is hard to understand. The editor marks these places with **proofreaders' marks**. Each mark has a special meaning, sort of like a code, and conveys a message to others who read the manuscript that a word may be spelled wrong, a new paragraph should be started, or other corrections should be made. The editor sends the marked-up manuscript to the author to see if she agrees with the changes. Soon a final typing of the story is made and no further changes will be made.

The editor looks at samples of the artist's work.

The Artist and the Designer

The Story Comes to Life

While reading the manuscript, the editor is also thinking about what sort of pictures to put with the story. She knows that good artwork can help express the ideas presented in the story, and it often makes the story more meaningful and fun to read. In her files, the editor keeps many samples of artwork from artists who are interested in **illustrating** children's books.

Looking through her files, the editor finds samples by a new artist. She likes how the artist's pictures seem to tell a story and how the artist drew the older characters. That would be important for drawing Gramma, the main character in Betsy's book. She asks one of the publishing company's book **designers** for his opinion on how this artist's style of drawing might fit with Betsy's story. Book designers work closely with editors to decide what sort of pictures to use in a book. The designer agrees with the editor's choice, and the editor sends a copy of the manuscript to the artist.

The artist reads the story and sketches a few scenes to give the editor and designer an idea of how she would draw the illustrations.

The sketches suit Betsy's story perfectly, and the editor hires the artist to illustrate *Green Beans*.

Next the artist prepares a book **dummy**. In publishing, a dummy is a model of the finished book. It begins as a blank book the same size and shape as the finished book will be. The artist makes sketches of all the illustrations, and then writes the story where it will fit on each page.

The dummy shows how the artist would like the final book to look. It also gives the editor and designer a chance to suggest changes before the artist makes the final drawings.

Now the artist can prepare the final artwork. From these photographs you can see how the original sketch of the grandmother developed into a sketch used in the dummy and finally into the color drawing.

The artist's finished pictures are just one element in the design of the finished book. While the final artwork is being prepared, the book designer looks at the dummy and sample sketches and chooses a **typeface** for the story. Some typefaces are very plain, while others can be fancy with lots of swirls and curls. For *Green Beans*, the designer looked at several typefaces that he thought fit the story and artwork. Then he looked at typefaces for the title of the book. None of the samples looked right to him, so he asked the artist to draw the letters in the title to look like green bean vines. That was just the right touch. It made the cover of the book a little more interesting than one of the standard typefaces would have.

The designer also looks at a large selection of papers that can be used for the final printing of the book. Some papers are smooth and shiny, and others are thick and rough. Some are inexpensive and others are expensive. There are hundreds of papers to choose from, so picking one takes some careful consideration.

When the completed artwork finally arrives, the editor and designer go over each piece. This is an exciting time; they can now see how the artist has expressed the author's ideas.

The Typesetter and the Keyliner

Words into Type...

So far, all the people who have worked on *Green Beans* have thought about the author's story and how they can help make it enjoyable to read and fun to look at. The rest of the people who work at making *Green Beans* a book have skills that are more technical. They may use sophisticated lasers and specialized computers to convert the words and pictures of the author and artist into the finished book.

The first specialized computer to be used in making *Green Beans* is the **typesetting** machine. In order to get perfectly shaped, solid black letters like the ones you see on this page, the story has to be typeset. To do this, the designer marks a copy of the manuscript with instructions about which typeface to use, how long each line of the story should be, and how big the letters should be. The designer sends this marked-up manuscript to the typesetter. The typesetter types in commands, or codes, so that the typesetting computer will make the type look the way the designer has specified. Sometimes a single word has a dozen different commands.

When all the information is entered into the computer, the typesetter hits the command to print. With a carefully controlled beam of light, the computer projects each letter in the text onto a special photographic paper that is similar to the paper that snapshots are printed on. After the paper is treated with photographic chemicals that make the letters visible and permanent, the paper is removed from the processing machine.

Each line of the story is printed just as it will look in the completed book. Some lines are printed at different lengths to allow the words to wrap around the artist's pictures.

...and Keeping Things Straight

After the type has been set and printed, a process called **keylining** takes place. A keyliner positions the type and illustrations on paper boards in the exact locations they will be in the finished book. Sometimes this is done by computer. *Green Beans*, however, was keylined by hand.

In a book with color illustrations, the keyliner first pastes down a black and white photocopy of the color artwork. This copy serves as a guide for pasting down the type that will accompany the artwork.

Here the keyliner pastes a section of type so that it wraps around the flowers in the illustration. If this isn't carefully done,

a line of type might end up crooked, like this one!

The completed board (correctly referred to as a "keyline" or "mechanical") is checked to make certain that everything is lined up perfectly.

Preparing to Print

Four-color Magic

With the keylines completed, the editor and designer can now see how each page of *Green Beans* is going to look. But what happens next to get from here to the printing press?

You might think of the printing press as being similar to a hand-held rubber stamp. On the bottom of a rubber stamp there might be a letter, words, or a picture. This picture is raised above the rubber base so when you press it onto an ink pad, just the raised part picks up the ink. When you press the stamp onto a piece of paper, the ink passes to the paper. To make *Green Beans* ready for the printing press, **printing plates** must be made. They work a lot like rubber stamps.

If all the words and pictures in *Green Beans* could be printed using only black ink, just one printing plate would be needed. It would work like a rubber stamp with a black ink pad. But what about the pictures? With all those different colors, how can a printing press have enough different colors of ink, each with its own printing plate, to make the pictures look the way the artist drew them? Well, something amazing takes place.

If you could look at the pictures in this book with a powerful magnifying glass, you would see that they are actually made up of tiny dots. These dots are printed using only four colors of ink: yellow, red, blue, and black. You probably already know that if you color a circle with a yellow crayon and then color over the yellow with a blue crayon, the circle will look green. Something similar happens when different combinations of yellow, red, blue, and black inks are mixed. The amazing thing is that by printing a combination of pinpoint-sized dots of these four **primary printing colors** (yellow, red, blue, and black), almost *any* color imaginable can be created. Using a printing press with just the primary printing colors to make pictures in full color is called **four-color process printing**.

This is what you would see if you had a powerful magnifying glass.

Four-color process printing will be used to make the pictures in *Green Beans*. The press will have four printing plates—one for each color of ink—that will print, one color on top of the other, to make full-color pictures. In order to make a printing plate for each of these colors, it is necessary to find out how much of each color is in the original artwork.

To find this out, the artwork is sent to a **color separator**. Here, a technician wraps the artwork around a drum in a computerized **laser scanning** machine. A beam of white light passes over, or scans, the artwork and makes a pinpoint-by-pinpoint analysis of the entire picture. Four scans are made—one for each color.

The technician then sets the machine to make four **negatives**. A laser beam exposes tiny dots onto a film similar to the kind of film that is used in cameras. One negative is made for each of the four printing inks.

Negatives look like the opposite of the original picture—they are light where the colors in the picture are dark and dark where the colors are light. For instance, the negative that was made by scanning for blue (we'll

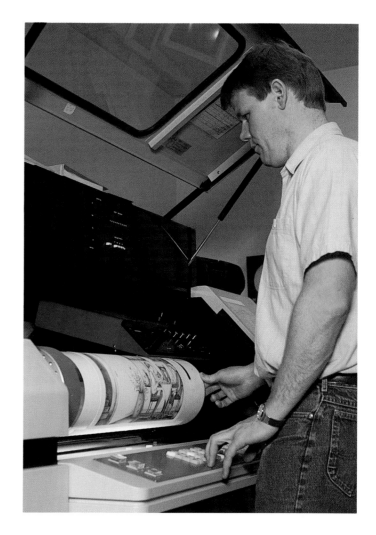

call it the "blue negative") is almost clear where it scanned the blue stripes on the white bowl of fruit. That's because the stripes are almost pure blue. The white bowl looks very dark on the blue negative, because there is no blue in the white bowl.

*The four sets of negatives
—one each for yellow, red,
blue, and black*

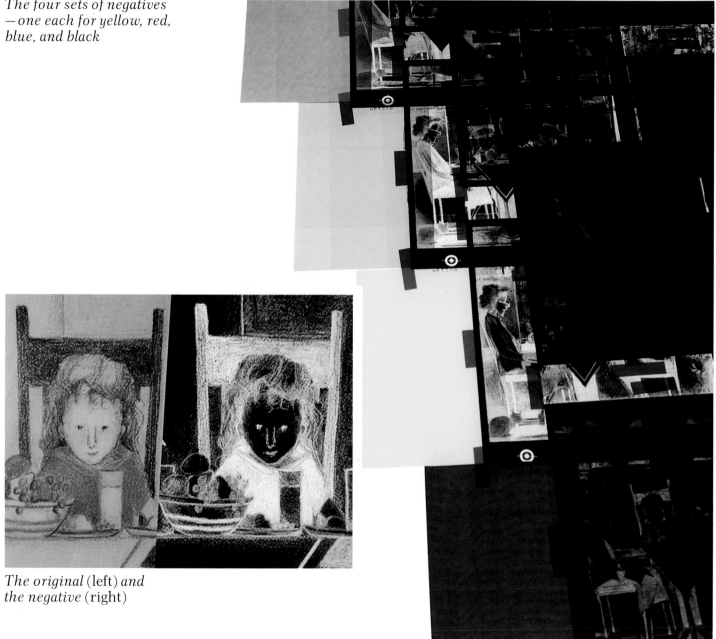

The original (left) *and
the negative* (right)

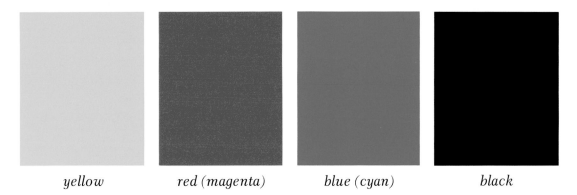

yellow   red (magenta)   blue (cyan)   black

The four colors used in four-color process printing are yellow, red, blue, and black. In order to get the best results, printers use a greenish shade of blue called cyan, and a purplish shade of red called magenta.

To make sure that the negatives are accurate, the color separator makes a **color proof**. The color proof is made up of four pieces of **acetate**, thin sheets of plastic that are coated with the same colors as the printing inks: yellow, red, blue, and black.

The separator starts with the blue negative. He lays it on top of the blue acetate and shines a bright light on them. Where the negative is clear, the light shines through onto the acetate. Where the negative is dark, the light does not shine through. Next, chemicals are poured onto the acetate. Anywhere the light shone on the acetate, it stays blue. Where the light was blocked by the dark areas of the negative, the blue coating washes away. The separator repeats this procedure for the other colors. Now the

separator has four pieces of acetate, one with the image of the artwork in blue, one in red, one in yellow, and one in black.

When these four pieces of acetate are precisely laid down, one on top of the other, the image appears once again in full color — like magic! These color proofs are checked over carefully because they show what the art will look like when it's printed. Sometimes a part of the art wasn't scanned properly and one of the colors will be too dark or too light. It's important to notice any mistakes now because once the printing press is started, it would be very expensive to stop it and wait for a new negative to be made.

These proofs look fine, so *Green Beans* moves on to the last step before printing.

In a process called **stripping**, the negatives are taped to large sheets of plastic called **flats**. The purpose of stripping is to put each page into the proper order for printing. Each sheet has eight negatives taped to it. There is one negative for each page and one flat for each of the four printing colors.

You can see that some of the negatives are attached right side up and others are upside down. This isn't a mistake! The printing press will print eight pages at once on big sheets of paper the same size as the flat. After each sheet is printed on both sides, the paper will be folded and all the pages will be right side up and in the proper order.

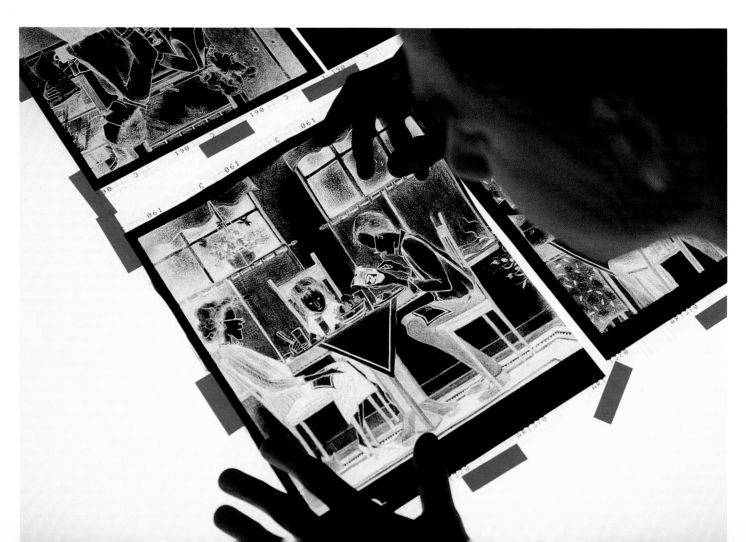

Finally, it's time to make the printing plates. This process is very much like the one used to make the color proofs, except that now the negatives will be exposed onto thin sheets of coated metal instead of colored acetate. One printing plate is made for each of the four colors to be printed.

First, the flats are laid on top of each plate and exposed to a very bright light. Then,

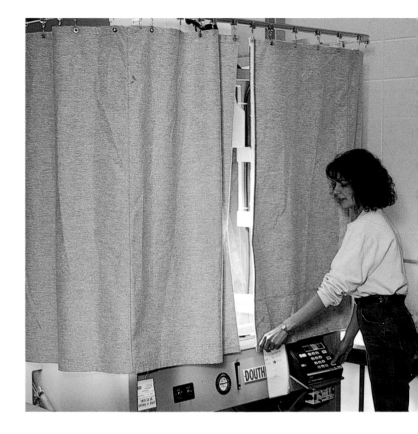

like the earlier proofs, when chemicals are poured over the plates, the coating washes away except where the light shone through. The images of each page of *Green Beans* appear on the metal. Like the raised part of the rubber stamp, these images hold the ink and pass it onto the paper in the printing press.

The completed printing plates for each of the four colors are given a final inspection.

At the Printer

Roll the Press!

After many months of careful preparation, *Green Beans* is ready to be printed. This is an exciting day for everyone. The author is excited to hear that her book is nearly finished; the artist is anxious to see her artwork in print; and the editor is eager to see the words and pictures on paper together.

The large four-color printing press is adjusted and made ready to run.

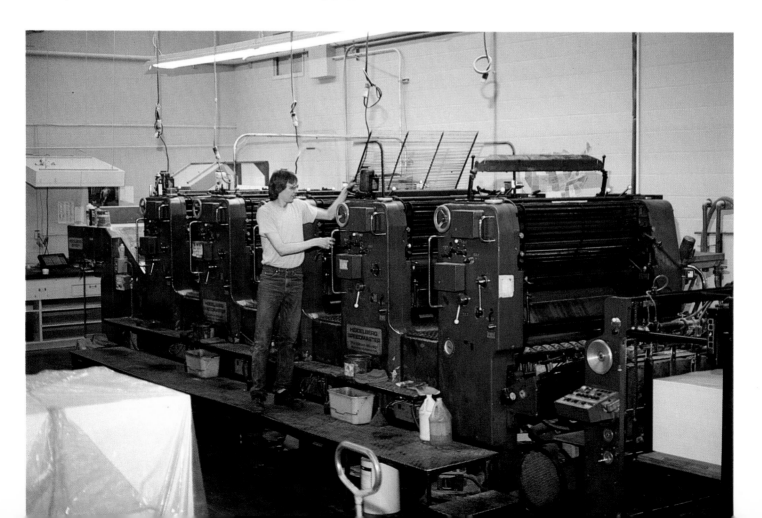

One of the plates is installed in the press.

Yellow, red, blue, and black inks are poured into their individual troughs. From here, the inks are transferred over a series of rollers to the printing plates.

Paper is loaded into one end of the press.

Like a giant waking up, the huge printing press comes to life. Slowly the powerful electric motors strain to bring the press up to operating speed. The printer listens to the press like a doctor listening to your heartbeat. When it sounds right, and the dials and gauges indicate that all is OK, the first sheets of paper are fed into the machine.

When everything is adjusted properly, the command is given to "Roll the press!"

The paper is printed with the blue and red inks from the first two plates. The image begins to appear.

Then the paper picks up the yellow ink and is finally printed with the black ink.

Here you can see the printing plate on top with a light coating of black ink. Like a rubber stamp, the printing plate picks up the ink only on the areas with pictures and words. The plate passes the ink to a rubber **blanket cylinder**, which then prints the ink onto the paper. Four colors completed!

Faster than you can say "green beans," a fully printed sheet pops out of the printing press. The printer pulls one of the sheets out of the growing stack and carefully checks to make certain that the colors are printing properly.

It takes just a few hours to print 10,000 sets of pages of *Green Beans*. After the ink is dry, the sheets are wrapped and shipped to a **bindery**.

At the Bindery

All Sewn Up

At the bindery, thousands of sheets of paper are transformed into books we can hold in our hands. To get to a finished book, however, each sheet of paper must go through a surprising number of steps.

First, the printed sheets are fed into the **folding** machine. Inside they are folded over and over again until they emerge as booklets called **signatures**.

The two signatures that make up *Green Beans* are loaded into a **gathering** machine, which gathers them together, along with the **endpapers**, in order. The endpapers are thick sheets of paper that are attached to the first and last pages of the book.

By looking at this unfolded signature, can you figure out how many times the paper was folded? Since *Green Beans* was printed on both sides of two sheets of paper, how many pages are there in the complete book? The answers are on page 48.

The gathering machine

Here you can see the second signature being pulled from its stack and sent down the line to be combined with the first signature.

Next, the two signatures are **sewn** together along the folded edge, called the **spine**, by a high-speed sewing machine. Sewing the signatures together makes the book very strong. These books will last for many years in homes, schools, and libraries. From here, the sewn signatures are fed into a powerful paper cutter to **trim** the excess paper along the edges.

A sturdy cover, or **case**, helps to protect the book and also makes it last longer. **Hardcover** books have stiff covers made from sheets of cardboard to which printed sheets of paper or cloth have been glued. **Paperback** books have flexible covers made from thick paper. They don't last as long as hardcovers since the covers can crease or tear, but they cost less to make and buy.

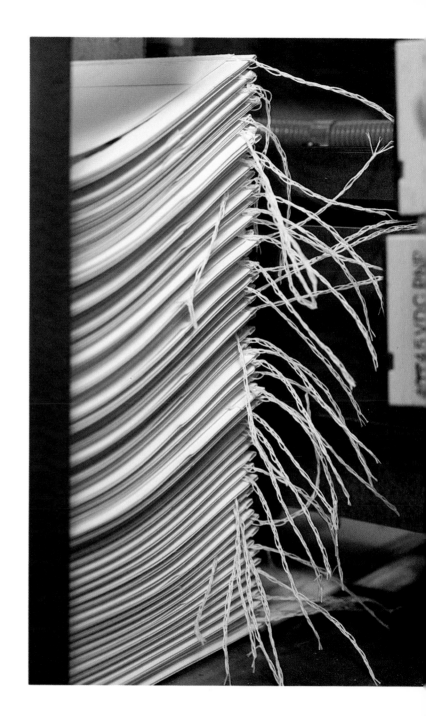

Two sewn signatures lie on top of a stack of thousands of completed covers. Stiff cardboard cores can be seen in the open covers.

Now it's time to complete the book. The final step is to attach the signatures to the covers. This is called **casing-in**. The casing-in machine applies glue to the covers and lays the signatures in the proper position along the glue line. As the covers and signatures move forward in the machine, the covers slide along a silver bar that flips them over. Rollers press the covers and signatures together to help the glue set properly. At the end of the line, the books are carefully stacked. Then they're sent to the warehouse for storage and shipping.

After nearly a year of careful preparation, *Green Beans* is at last a book. Betsy's experiences as a young girl helping her grandmother in the garden can now be shared with others. It took dozens of skilled people to make her idea into a shared idea . . . into a very special book.

Now schools, libraries, and bookstores all across the country will order *Green Beans* from the publisher. Who knows—it might even be in your library!

Glossary

acetate: a thin sheet of colored plastic that is used to make color proofs

blanket cylinder: a rubber-covered roller in the printing press that transfers ink from the printing plate onto the paper

book publisher: a company that creates books, or the head of that company

casing-in: attaching the cover, or case, to the pages of the book in the binding process

color proof: four sheets of acetate—one for each of the printing inks—that are laid one on top of the other to show how the original image will look when printed

color separation: the process of separating the primary printing colors from the original artwork

designer: the person who decides how the book will look, for example, by choosing the typeface and working with the illustrator

dummy: a handmade model of the finished book

editor: the person responsible for guiding the manuscript through the publishing process

endpapers: thick sheets of paper that are glued onto the inside covers of the book and connect the pages of the book to the cover

flats: sheets of plastic with the film for each page of the book taped in the proper position for printing

folding: a part of the binding process, the printed sheet is folded into a booklet called a signature

four-color process printing: printing yellow, red, blue, and black dots to create a full color image that looks like a color photograph or artwork

gathering: assembling the signatures in the proper order for binding

hardcover: a book with a stiff cover

illustrate: to make pictures for a story

keylining: putting the type and illustrations in the correct position for each page of the book

laser-scanning: the use of intense beams of light to re-create images on film

manuscript: the written or typed version of a story

negative: film that shows the opposite of the original image, so that wherever the original image is dark, the negative is light, and wherever the original image is light, the negative is dark

paperback: a book with a soft paper cover

primary printing colors: in printing, the primary colors are yellow, red, blue, and black. These colors can be printed together to create almost any color. (In order to get the best results, printers use a greenish shade of blue called cyan, and a purplish shade of red called magenta.)

printing plate: a sheet of metal onto which the image to be printed is exposed

proofreaders' marks: handwritten symbols that indicate mistakes or changes

sewn: a very strong type of binding in which the pages are stitched together along the spine

signature: a printed sheet that has been folded and looks like a booklet

spine: the back of a bound book that connects the front and back covers

stripping: taping negatives on flats in the proper position for printing

trimming: cutting the excess paper to make the finished edges of a book

typesetting: using a machine to create perfectly formed letters and words like the ones you see on this page

typeface: one of many styles of letters used by typesetting machines

---

Answers to questions on page 41:
The photograph shows a printed sheet that has been folded three times. Eight pages have been printed on each side, so there are sixteen pages altogether on each sheet. *Green Beans* is made up of two sheets, so *Green Beans* is 32 pages long.